CAROUSELS

Senior Author
William K. Durr

Senior Coordinating Author
John J. Pikulski

Coordinating Authors
Rita M. Bean
J. David Cooper
Nicholas A. Glaser
M. Jean Greenlaw
Hugh Schoephoerster

Authors
Mary Lou Alsin
Kathryn Au
Rosalinda B. Barrera
Joseph E. Brzeinski
Ruth P. Bunyan

Jacqueline C. Comas
Frank X. Estrada
Robert L. Hillerich
Timothy G. Johnson
Pamela A. Mason
Joseph S. Renzulli

HOUGHTON MIFFLIN COMPANY   BOSTON

Atlanta   Dallas   Geneva, Illinois   Palo Alto   Princeton   Toronto

Acknowledgments

For each of the selections listed below, grateful acknowledgment is made for permission to adapt and/or reprint original or copyrighted material, as follows:

"Autumn Wind," by Helen Howland Prommel. Copyright © 1943 by The Curtis Publishing Company. Reprinted by permission of Harold Prommel.

"Beatrice," from *Beatrice Doesn't Want To,* by Laura Joffe Numeroff. Copyright © 1981 by Laura Joffe Numeroff. Adapted and reprinted by permission of Franklin Watts.

"The Big Mile Race," from *The Big Mile Race,* by Leonard Kessler. Copyright © 1983 by Leonard Kessler. Entire text adapted and reprinted by permission of Greenwillow Books (A Division of William Morrow & Company).

"Clyde Monster," from *Clyde Monster,* by Robert L. Crowe. Text Copyright © 1976 by Robert L. Crowe. Adapted and reprinted by permission of the publisher, E. P. Dutton, a division of New American Library.

"The Dinosaurs' Dinner," by Dennis Lee from *Alligator Pie Calendar* by Dennis Lee and Frank Newfield. Reprinted by permission of Macmillan of Canada, A Division of Gage Publishing Limited.

Continued on page 264.

Contents

Magazine One

12 **Beatrice**
by Laura Joffe Numeroff

25 Skill: **Alphabetical Order**

29 Reading for Information:
A Special Place

34 **The Big Mile Race**
by Leonard Kessler

51 **Race**
a poem by B. J. Lee

52 Vocabulary: **Opposites**

53 **Sports Day**

66 **We Are Best Friends**
by Aliki

81 **The Tadpole**
a poem by E. E. Gould

82 Magazine Wrap-up

Magazine Two

88 **Harriet and the Garden**
by Nancy Carlson

100 Vocabulary: Multiple-meaning
Words
Which Meaning?

4

101 Reading for Information:
What Can You Do with a Yam?

106 **Nate the Great and
the Lost Stamp**
by Marjorie Weinman Sharmat

131 **The Dinosaurs' Dinner**
a poem by Dennis Lee

132 Skill: **The Main Idea**

136 **The Little Pine Tree**
a play

159 **Autumn Wind**
a poem
by Helen Howland Prommel

160 Magazine Wrap-up

Magazine Three

166 **What Mary Jo Shared**
by Janice May Udry

187 **Umbrellas**
a poem
by Barbara Juster Esbensen

188 **Clyde Monster**
by Robert L. Crowe

201 **Night Comes**
a poem
by Beatrice Schenk de Regniers

202 Vocabulary: **Describing Words**

203 Reading for Information:
Animal Homes

208 **Good As New**
by Barbara Douglass

224 Skill: Decoding Strategy
Reading New Words

228 Medallion Selection:
The Man and His Caps

242 Magazine Wrap-up

244 **Picture Dictionary**

253 **Student Handbook**

Carousels
Magazine One

Contents

Stories

12 **Beatrice**
Laura Joffe Numeroff

34 **The Big Mile Race**
Leonard Kessler

53 **Sports Day**

66 **We Are Best Friends**
Aliki

Article

29 **A Special Place**

Poems

51 **Race**
B. J. Lee

81 **The Tadpole**
E. E. Gould

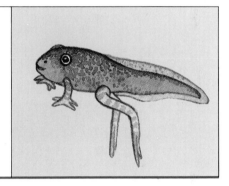

Skill

25 **Alphabetical Order**

Vocabulary

52 **Opposites**

82 Magazine Wrap-up

Beatrice

by Laura Joffe Numeroff

Beatrice does not like books,
and she does not like the library.
Will Beatrice still feel that way
after three days at the library?

Beatrice didn't like books.

She didn't like to read.

She didn't like to go to the library.

But that's where her brother Henry had to take her on three days.

Henry had work to do at the library, and he had to look after Beatrice.

13

"Why don't you get some books,"
Henry said when they got to the library.

"I don't want to," said Beatrice.

"Look at how many books there are!"
Henry said.

"I don't want to," Beatrice told him.

"Then what do you want to do?" Henry asked.

"I want to see what you do," said Beatrice.

"But I have to work," said Henry.

"That's OK," Beatrice said.

"I give up," said Henry at last.
He started working and didn't look at his sister.

The next day Beatrice didn't want to go into the library.

"Come on, Bea," said her brother.

"I don't want to," Beatrice told him.

"But I have to work," said Henry.

"I'll wait here," Beatrice decided.

"OK," said Henry, "but wait for me."

Beatrice said she would wait.

Henry was working in the library.
All at once he could feel water.
Henry looked around.
There was Beatrice.
"It's raining," she told her brother.

"I give up," said Henry.

It was still raining on the last day.
Beatrice *had* to go in this time
to get out of the rain.

Henry got some books.

"May I help?" Beatrice asked.

Henry gave her some books.

"They are too big!" Beatrice said, and all the books fell.

"I give up!" said Henry. "I don't know what to do with you! Look, Bea, I have to do my work!"

"Henry," asked Beatrice, "do you think I could have some water?"

So they went to look for some water.

On the way Henry saw a sign.

"Come on," Henry said.

"I don't want to," said Beatrice.

"You have to!" said Henry.

Soon Beatrice was in a room
with many children.

A woman started to read,
"Alfred Mouse lived in a new house."
Beatrice looked out the window
next to her.

The woman read some more,
"Alfred Mouse had new skates."
Beatrice liked to skate.
"But Alfred's mother didn't like it
when he skated in the house,"
read the woman.
The children laughed.

Beatrice thought about the time
she had skated in her house.

Then at last Beatrice laughed.
She wanted to know all about Alfred.

When the story was over,
Beatrice asked, "May I see that book?"

"Oh, yes," said the woman.
Beatrice looked at the book.

Henry came to get Beatrice.
"Time to go," he said to her.
Beatrice didn't stop reading.

Henry put Beatrice's hat on her.
"We have to go home now," he said.
Beatrice didn't look at her brother.

"Come on, Bea," Henry said.

"I don't want to," Beatrice said.

Story Wrap-up

Summary Questions

At first, Beatrice didn't like the library. She didn't feel the same way on the last day.

The questions will help you tell why.

1. What things showed that Beatrice didn't like the library?
2. What made her like it?
3. What do you think Beatrice will do when she goes back to the library? Name some books you think Beatrice would like.

The Reading and Writing Connection

Beatrice likes books now.

What if she had a friend who didn't like books?

Be Beatrice.

Tell what you would say and do to help your friend like books.

The words in the box can help you.

library	**mouse**	**skates**
woman	**brother**	**rain**

Alphabetical Order

Here is the alphabet.

A B C D E F G H I J K L M
N O P Q R S T U V W X Y Z

You know how to say the letters
of the alphabet in order.

The names and words in some books
are in the order of the alphabet.
They are in alphabetical order.
If you want to find a name or
word in one of these books, you have
to know about alphabetical order.

The names of these children are
in alphabetical order.

<u>A</u> is the first letter of the alphabet.

<u>Alma</u> begins with <u>A</u>, so <u>Alma</u> is first.

<u>B</u> is the next letter of the alphabet.

<u>Beth</u> begins with <u>B</u>, so <u>Beth</u> is next.

Why is <u>Caleb</u> next?

Why is <u>Dan</u> last?

Look at this row of words.

Put the words in alphabetical order.

dark   again   cry   brother

These names are in alphabetical order, too.

None of the names begins with A.

B is the next letter of the alphabet, so Ben is first.

None of the names begins with C, D, or E.

F is the next letter of the alphabet, so Fred is after Ben.

Why is Lisa after Fred?

Why is Pam last?

Use what you know to put this row of words in alphabetical order.

turtle   fish   pig   bear

Here are some more words.

Use what you know to put each row of words in alphabetical order.

Row 1: **does   about   coat   both**
Row 2: **last   water   dog   or**

A Special Place

What if you wanted to know about dogs, rabbits, or bears?

Where could you go to find books about them?

You could go to the library!

You can find storybooks in the library, too.

Sometimes you go to the library
to get one special storybook.

Storybooks are placed
in alphabetical order.

The last names of the authors
are used to put them in that order.

Maybe you want to read a book
about Curious George.

How would you find that book?

First you need to know that
the author of the book *Curious George*
is H. A. Rey.

You would have to find books
by authors who have last names
beginning with an R.

A book about Curious George
should be there.

When you have your book,
you should go to the librarian.

The librarian will mark your book
or a card.

The mark will let you know
when you should bring back your book.

Now go home and have fun reading!

Summary Questions

The questions will help you tell what you found out about the library.

1. How can you find a storybook in the library?
2. Why does the librarian mark the books?
3. If you were an author, how would someone find your book in the library?

The Reading and Writing Connection

Would you like to be an author?
Tell what you would write about.
The words in the box may help you.

author	**special**	**library**
book	**librarian**	**write**

The Big Mile Race

by Leonard Kessler

There is going to be a big race.
How will Frog do in the race?

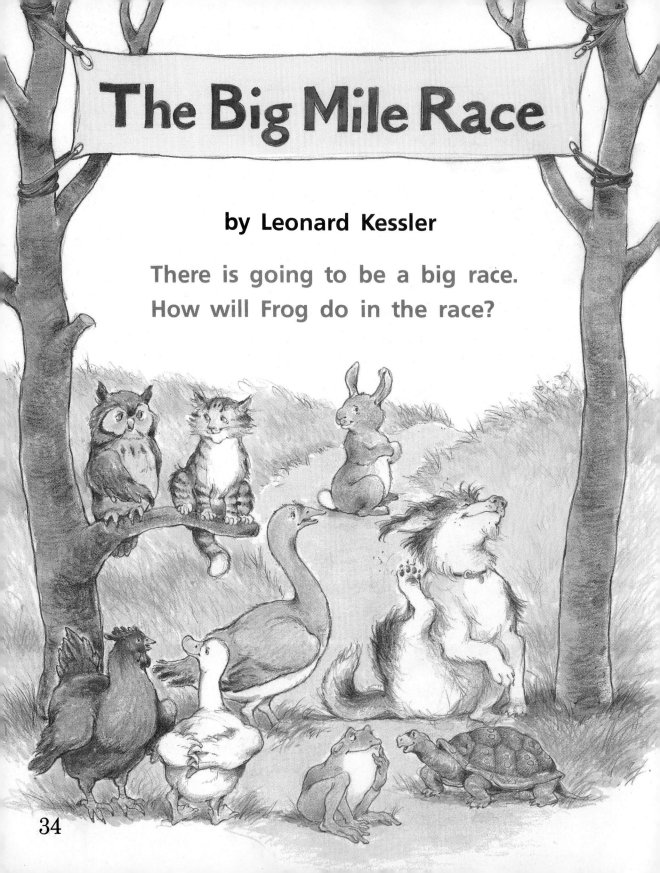

"Look at that sign," said Duck.

"What sign?" asked Hen.

"There," said Goose.

Frog read the sign to everyone.

Big Mile Race
Sign up today
at the tree
by the rocks.

"I want to be in the race," said Dog.

"I do, too," said Goose.

"I want to run a mile," said Hen.

"I want to be in the big
mile race, too," said Frog.

"You can't *run*," said Duck.
"You can only hop."

"Then Frog will hop
for a mile," said Cat.

At the tree by the rocks, they saw Rabbit and Turtle.

"We want to run in the big race," said Duck.

"May I hop in the race?" Frog asked.

"You may if you want," said Rabbit.

"Good!" shouted Frog.

"Well, you won't finish," said Duck.

"Frog will finish," said Hen.

"Sign up over here," said Turtle.

Owl said, "We all have work to do.
We have to get ready for the race.
We need to run every day."

"And *hop!*" said Frog.

"And HOP!" Owl said.

Every day they worked hard.
At last they were ready for the race.

"Get up, Duck," Frog called.
"Today is the big mile race."

"Do you still want to be
in the race?" asked Duck.

"Oh, yes," said Frog.

"You can't win," said Duck.

"Maybe I can't win," Frog said.
"But I'm going to hop to the finish."

39

All the runners went to the rocks.
"Everyone warm up," said Owl.

"I don't need to warm up,"
said Goose.

"Look here, everyone," said Rabbit.
"The race will start here
and it will finish there.
The first one at the finish wins."

Then Turtle called, "Everyone ready?
One, two, three, GO!"

Goose was first.
Owl was next.
Cat was after Owl.
Then came the other runners.

Where was Frog?
He was last.

The racers ran and ran.
Goose was still first,
but she was slowing down.

When they got to some trees,
Owl was first.

Goose was next.

Dog was after Goose.

"I need to stop," Goose told Hen.

"You did not warm up," Hen called.

When they went by the pond,
Cat was first.

Owl was next.

Dog was after Owl.

Then came the other racers.

Who was last?

It was Frog.

But he was still hopping.

Where was Goose?

Goose was in the pond.

"I can't finish the race,"
Goose called to Hen.
"Next time I will warm up."

Owl was slowing down.
Duck was slowing down, too.
"Where is Frog?" Duck asked.

"I am back here," Frog called.

"Keep hopping!" Hen shouted.

"Here comes the big hill," said Owl.

Duck ran up the hill.
She went up the hill so fast
that she ran by Owl, Cat, and Dog.

"I'm first!" Duck shouted.

Duck looked back — and fell down.
"Oh, no!" she said.
But soon Duck was running again.

"Where is Frog?" asked Hen.

"I don't see him," said Duck.

Rabbit and Turtle waited
at the finish.

"Here comes Dog," shouted Rabbit.
"She's the winner!"

Then one by one the other runners
finished the race.

"Where is Frog?" asked Rabbit.

"Maybe he stopped," said Turtle.

"No! I see Frog," said Cat.

"Keep hopping!" called Dog.

"You can do it!" Duck shouted.

Frog hopped to the finish.

"You did it!" said Hen.

"I finished," said Frog,
"but I finished last."

"We lost, too," said Duck and Hen.

"But we *finished* the big mile race,"
said Frog.
"That's what counts!"

"Next time we will run faster,"
Duck said.

"HOP FASTER!" shouted Frog,
"and maybe next time *I'll* be first!"

Summary Questions

Frog wanted to hop in the race.
The questions can help you tell why.

1. Frog knew that he couldn't win.
   Why did he want to be in the race?
2. Do you think Frog was pleased
   with himself in the race?
   Why do you think that?
3. Do you think Frog can ever win
   a mile race? Why or why not?
4. Draw a picture map for the race.
   Show which way the racers went
   before they got to the finish line.

The Reading and Writing Connection

Frog wants to have a hopping race.
How would you help Frog get ready?
Write some sentences that tell
what you would say to Frog.
The words in the box will help you.

start	**faster**	**goose**	**finish**
hop	**shout**	**hill**	**warm up**

Big Mile Race
Sign up today
at the tree
by the rocks.

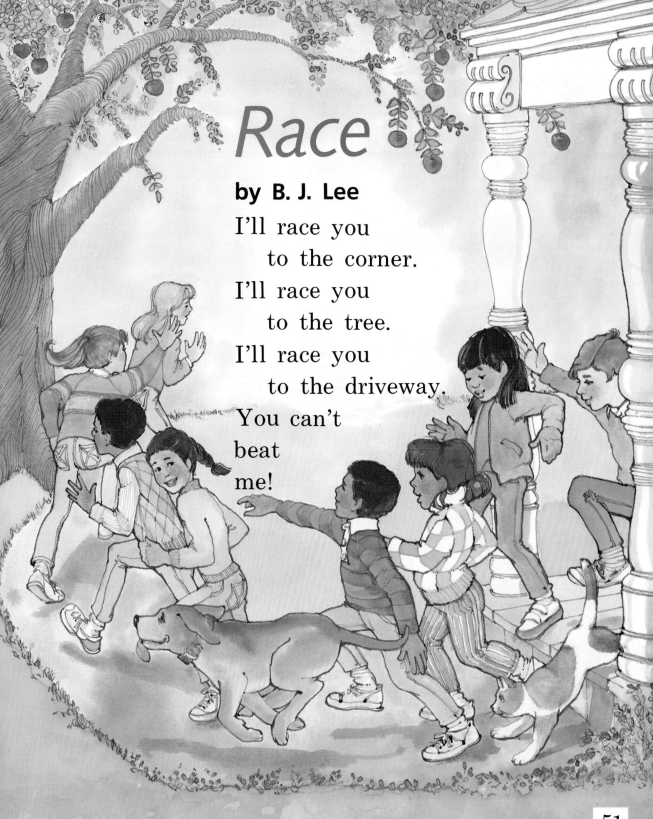

Race

by B. J. Lee

I'll race you
    to the corner.
I'll race you
    to the tree.
I'll race you
    to the driveway.
You can't
beat
me!

Opposites

A fox is walking up the hill.
A cat is walking down the hill.
Up is the opposite of **down**.
The fox and the cat are going
opposite ways.

Big and **little** are opposites.
Laugh and **cry** are opposites, too.

Finish some sentences with opposites.
1. The rabbit is **fast.**
    The turtle is _____ . **cute   slow**
2. One sign says **in.**
    One sign says _____ . **out   stop**

Sports Day

Lisa likes games.
Today Lisa is going to a ball game.
Find out about all the good things
that happen at the game.

"We are having Sports Day
at school," Lisa said to her dad.
"I have to do a report about a sport.
I can't decide what to tell about."

"I'll help you think of something
after supper," said Dad.
"Now I have a surprise for you.
You know that the Bears have
an important game today.
Well, we are going to that game."

"Oh, great!" shouted Lisa.

Then she said, "I know!

I can be a reporter and tell about this game on Sports Day."

Then Lisa went to get the sign that she took to every game.

It was for the player she liked best, Henry Wills.

If the Bears could win today's game,
they would be in first place.

This was a very important ball game.

Lisa thought the Bears could win.

She said to her dad, "They played
a great game the other day.

If they can play like that today,
they should win."

At the game, Lisa and her dad sat in back of the Bears.

They would have no problem seeing the game.

At last the ball game started.

Lisa held up her sign and shouted, "Go, Henry, go!"

The other players, the Owls,
were up at bat first.
They made one home run.
Then the Bears were up at bat.
The first player made a home run!

Lisa took pictures of the ball game.
She didn't want to forget a thing.

Soon it was the last time
for the Owls to be up at bat.
They had five runs,
and so did the Bears.

But the Owls couldn't get a hit.
Now the Bears were going to bat.
They needed to hit one home run.

Henry Wills was the first one up.
The ball raced at Henry.
He hit a home run!
The Bears were now in first place!

"Lisa!" said Dad.
"We should talk to Henry Wills."

Before going down to the players,
Lisa wanted to show her sign again.
She started to put up her sign,
but somehow she let go of it.
The sign fell down on Henry Wills!

Henry read the sign and laughed.

He looked up and saw Lisa.

He held up the sign and asked,
"Is this your sign?"

"Yes," said Lisa.

"Thank you for getting it."

Then she said, "I'm doing a report
about this game.

May I talk with you?"

"Yes," said Henry.

The first thing Lisa asked was,
"How did you get to be the best?"

"I have worked at it,"
said Henry.
"Sometimes it was all work.
But many times it is fun, too.
Today was one of the fun times!"

Lisa talked some more with Henry.
Then she said, "I should let you go.
Thanks, Mr. Wills."

"Wait!" said Henry.
He got a ball and signed it.
"This is for you," he said.

"Thanks, Mr. Wills!" said Lisa.

Then Dad took the best picture
of the game.
It was a picture of Lisa
with Henry Wills.

Summary Questions

Lisa had a great day at the game.
The questions will help you tell why.

1. Why did Lisa decide to write
   a report about the ball game?
2. How did Lisa show that she liked
   Henry Wills best of all?
3. Lisa's sign fell.
   How did this help her with her report?
4. What was the best thing
   about Lisa's day at the ball game?
   Why do you think that?

The Reading and Writing Connection

Lisa felt important when she gave her report and showed the picture.

Do you think Henry Wills will sign the picture for Lisa?

Why would he do this?

Write some sentences that you think Henry Wills would write on the back of the picture.

The words in the box can help you.

sports	**important**	**game**	**hit**
talk	**great**	**best**	**bat**

We Are Best Friends

by Aliki

Robert and Peter are best friends.
But then Peter has to move.
See if Robert gets a new friend.

Peter came to tell Robert the news.
"I am moving away," Peter said.

"You can't move away," said Robert.
"We are best friends.
What will you do without me?
Who will you play with?"

"I will live in a new house,"
said Peter.

"I will be going to a new school.
I will make new friends."

"You can't move away," said Robert.
"You will miss me too much."
But Peter moved away.

There was no fun without Peter.
There was no one to play with.
There was no one to share with,
not the way best friends share.

One day at school a boy said,
"My name is Will.

I come from another school."

"I don't like him," thought Robert.

"My friends are all there," said Will.

"I don't like silly names like Will,"
thought Robert.

"It was fun there," said Will.
"This place isn't much fun at all."

Then a letter came for Robert.
It was a letter from Peter.

Dear Robert,

I like my new house now.

I like my new school now.

At first I didn't like a thing, but now I have a friend, Alex.

You are my best friend, but Alex is nice, too.

It is fun to have someone to play with again.

Love,

Peter

Robert drew Peter a letter.
He drew two boys playing.
He wrote:

**If you were here, this is what
we would be doing.
But you are not here.**

Then he wrote:

There is a new boy in school.

Robert saw Will by a fence.
"Are you looking for something?"
Robert asked.

"I thought I saw a frog," said Will.
"I like frogs.
I used to have a frog named Greenie.
He would wait for me at the pond
by my house.
He must miss me very much."

"I know where there are frogs,"
said Robert.

"There are some by my house.
You can see for yourself."

"If I had a frog by my house,
I would share it," said Will.

"That's what I'm doing," said Robert.

Robert and Will went to see
the frogs at Robert's house.

One jumped, and Will got it.

"I'll call you Greenie, too," he said.

Robert said, "My friend Peter used
to come see the tadpoles.

He called the tadpoles Inkywiggles.

He must miss the tadpoles."

"Why?" asked Will.

"Peter moved away," said Robert.
"I write him letters."

"Then you can write
about the Inkywiggles," said Will.
    They laughed.
"This is the first time I have had
so much fun here," said Will.

"I'm having fun, too," said Robert.

Robert wrote to Peter.

Dear Peter,

   I can't wait for you to come see me.
   The new boy is called Will.
   I showed him the frogs.
   He had a frog by his other home,
but he had to move away, like you.
   He likes the name Inkywiggles.
                    Love,
                    Robert
   P.S. How is Alex?
   P.P.S. See you soon.

When the letter was finished,
Robert went out.
   He was going over
to Will's house to play.

Story Wrap-up

Summary Questions

Robert's friend Peter moved away, but they are still friends.

They each have a new friend, too.

These questions can help you tell how this happened.

1. Why did Robert tell Peter that he couldn't move away? What did Peter say?
2. How did Robert and Will become friends?
3. Why do you think Peter made a new friend before Robert did?
4. One day Peter will come to see Robert. Tell what you think they will do.

The Reading and Writing Connection

Robert wrote the last letter.
Now Peter wants to write back.
Make believe that you are Peter.
Write a letter back to Robert.
Tell how you feel.
Share some news.
The words in the box can help you.

move	**share**	**Dear**	**drew**
away	**tadpoles**	**Love**	**wrote**

The Tadpole

by E. E. Gould

Underneath the water-weeds
Small and black, I wriggle,
And life is most surprising!
Wiggle! waggle! wiggle!
There's every now and then a most
Exciting change in me,
I wonder, wiggle! waggle!
What I *shall* turn out to be!

Magazine Wrap-up

Do You Remember?

1. Something important happened
   to Beatrice, to Frog, to Lisa,
   and to Robert.
   What important thing happened
   to each of them?
2. Frog, Lisa, and Robert all had friends.
   Name their friends.

Writing about a Story

Write the name of the story that you liked best.

Write some sentences that tell why you liked it.

Books to Enjoy

Jump, Frog, Jump by Robert Kalan
Find out how some fast jumping helps a frog.

Margie and Me by Beverly Wirth
Here are three stories about a girl and her dog.

Do Pigs Sit in Trees? by Jean Zelasney
This story is about a pig who looks in some silly places for his mother.

Carousels
Magazine Two

Contents

Stories

88 Harriet and the Garden
Nancy Carlson

**106 Nate the Great and
the Lost Stamp**
Marjorie Weinman Sharmat

Play

136 The Little Pine Tree

Article

101 What Can You Do with a Yam?

Poems

131 **The Dinosaurs' Dinner**
Dennis Lee

159 **Autumn Wind**
Helen Howland Prommel

Skill
132 **The Main Idea**

Vocabulary: Multiple-meaning Words
100 **Which Meaning?**

160 Magazine Wrap-up

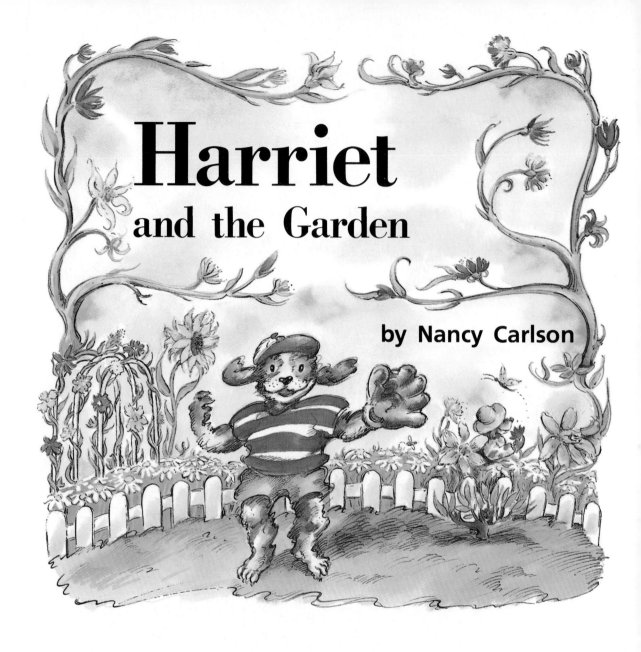

Harriet
and the Garden

by Nancy Carlson

Harriet runs into Mrs. Hoozit's garden.
What will Harriet do about the garden?
How will that make her feel?

It was a great day.
Harriet was playing ball
with some friends.

Mrs. Hoozit was working
in her flower garden.

Mrs. Hoozit had waited for
just this day.

One of her flowers looked great.

She thought that it could win
a garden prize.

"I must go and make a call,"
she said.

"I must have someone come over
to look at my prize flower."

As Mrs. Hoozit was making her call,
Harriet and her friends were playing.
All at once George hit a fly ball.
Harriet just had to get it.
If she didn't, it would be a home run.

As Harriet ran back and back,
she thought only about the ball.
She was thinking so hard
that she didn't know when she came
to Mrs. Hoozit's garden.

Harriet ran back right
into all the flowers.

Just as she got the ball, she fell
on the prize flower.

"Oh, oh," said Harriet.

"Let's get out of here!"
said her friends.

Everyone ran but Harriet.
She looked around her at the garden.
Everything was a mess.

All at once Mrs. Hoozit called out, "What's happened to my garden?"

Harriet was so scared that she just ran away.

She ran and she ran, and she didn't look back even once.

Harriet ran all the way home and up into her bedroom.

"Maybe she didn't see me," thought Harriet.

"Are you feeling all right, Harriet?" Mother asked.

"Just great," said Harriet.
But Harriet wasn't feeling great.

That night Harriet couldn't eat.
She didn't even look when Mother
made something she loved.

When Harriet went to bed,
she couldn't get to sleep.
When at last she did go to sleep,
she didn't sleep well at all.

The next day Harriet decided
what she had to do.

She went right over
to Mrs. Hoozit's house.

She told Mrs. Hoozit
what had happened.

Then, all that day, Harriet helped
Mrs. Hoozit plant new flowers.

They had a good time.

When Harriet got home,
she was a mess.

"Harriet, are you feeling all right?"
Mother asked.

"Just great!" said Harriet.
And Harriet *was* feeling great.

Summary Questions

Harriet had a big problem.
These questions will help you tell
what happened and how Harriet felt.

1. Did Harriet mean to mess up
   Mrs. Hoozit's garden?
   How did it happen?
2. How did Harriet feel that night?
   What helped you know that?
3. Harriet decided that she *had* to go
   back to see Mrs. Hoozit.
   Why do you think she felt that way?
4. Do you think Harriet and Mrs. Hoozit
   will be friends now? Why or why not?

The Reading and Writing Connection

Harriet helped Mrs. Hoozit plant more flowers.

Draw Mrs. Hoozit's new garden.

Use as many colors as you can.

Decide which flower is the best.

Write about why that flower should win a prize.

The words in the box can help you.

flower	**garden**	**prize**
	color	**great**

Which Meaning?

Some words have more than one meaning.

Read these sentences.

1. Robert hit a **fly** ball.
2. A **fly** is on the flower.

The other words in these sentences help you to know which meaning for **fly** is being used.

Now decide which sentence tells about each of the pictures.

1. I have a ball and a **bat**.
2. The **bat** is flying away.

1. He moved a **rock**.
2. Don't **rock** the boat.

What Can You Do with a Yam?

What can you do with a yam?

If you are hungry, you can eat it.

If you put it in water,
you can grow it.

Let's see how you can grow a yam.

Find a jar that's not too big
or too little.

Put some warm water into the jar.

Cut away a little of the yam.

Then push a stick into the yam,
but don't push it in *all* the way.

Now push in three more sticks.

Put the yam into the jar
with the cut part down.
Place the jar next to a window.
In two or three days, the water
in the jar will go down.
Then you must put in more water.

You'll have to wait a while,
but at last a plant will start to grow.

A yam plant can grow to be
a very big plant.

Who knows?

Your yam plant could grow into
a great big prize plant!

Summary Questions

The questions will help you tell about growing a yam plant.

1. What things do you need to grow a plant from a yam?
2. What do you do with the things?
3. Will you grow a yam plant? Tell about it.

The Reading and Writing Connection

Make believe your yam plant grows as big as a house!
Write a story about your plant.
Tell what would happen.
The words in the box can help you.

grow	stick	part	yam

Nate the Great
and the Lost Stamp

by Marjorie Weinman Sharmat
Part 1

Nate is great at finding lost things.
Find out what he does
as he looks for a lost stamp.

I, Nate the Great, was reading
a detective book when Claude
came over.

"I lost my dinosaur," Claude said.

I asked, "How could you do that?
A dinosaur is very big."

"My dinosaur is little," Claude said.
"It is a dinosaur on a stamp.
Can you help me find it?"

"This will be a hard case," I said, "but I will take it.

Where was the dinosaur stamp the last time you saw it?"

"It was in my house," Claude said. "I was showing all my stamps to Annie, Pip, and Rosamond."

I said, "I, Nate the Great, will go to your house."

I wrote a note to my mother.

Dear Mother,
I am on a sticky case.
When I find something big
that is little, I will be back.
Love,
Nate the Great

Claude and I went to his house.

"Here are all my other stamps,"
Claude said.

I, Nate the Great, saw many stamps.
I showed a stamp to Sludge.
"We must look for a stamp," I said.

Sometimes Sludge is not
a great detective.
Sludge wanted to lick the stamp.
He wanted to lick the sticky side.
"*Look*. Don't lick," I said.

Sludge and I looked everywhere.
We did not find the dinosaur stamp.
I asked Claude, "When did you
know the stamp was missing?"

"After everyone left," he said.

"Did everyone go
at the same time?" I asked.

"Yes," said Claude.

"Did everyone come over
at the same time?" I asked.

"No," said Claude.

"Annie and Rosamond came to say that Rosamond was having a sale.

Then it started to rain.

It rained for a long time, so Annie and Rosamond looked at my stamps.

When the rain stopped, Pip came by.

He looked at my stamps, too.

Then they all left to go to Rosamond's sale."

"Then I, Nate the Great, must go to the sale, too," I said.

Sludge and I went to see Rosamond.
"Do you have a dinosaur stamp?"
I asked Rosamond.

"No," she said, "but Claude does."

"Thank you," I said.
I started to leave.

Then I saw Pip.

"Did you see a dinosaur stamp at Claude's house?" I asked Pip.

Pip doesn't say much.

He moved his head up and down.

"Do you know where it is now?" I asked.

Pip moved his head sideways.

"Thank you," I said.

I saw Annie and her dog Fang.

"I am looking for Claude's dinosaur stamp," I said.

"What do you know about it?"

"I know that it looks like Fang," Annie said.

Then she said to Fang, "Show us your dinosaur smile."

Fang smiled.

I, Nate the Great, knew that it was time to leave.

I said good-by to Annie.

Summary Questions

These questions will help you tell what happened when Nate started to look for Claude's stamp.

1. What did Nate do to find the stamp? What did he find out?
2. Do you think it was a good idea for Claude to ask Nate for help? Why?

The Reading and Writing Connection

What would a sign say if Nate made it to help find the lost stamp?

Make a sign for Nate.

The words in the box can help you.

stamp	dinosaur	sticky
	case	detective

Nate the Great and the Lost Stamp

by Marjorie Weinman Sharmat

Part 2

Nate still hasn't
found the stamp.
See if he will find it.

Sludge and I walked home.
I saw myself in puddles.

At home I made something to eat.
I thought about the dinosaur stamp.
Should I think about the dinosaur
or about the stamp?
"I have to find out more
about dinosaurs," I said to Sludge.

I went to see some dinosaurs.

I found a dinosaur to look at.
I looked up ... and up ... and up.
It was big, but it could not move.
I, Nate the Great, was happy
about that.
I found out all about the dinosaur,
but that did not help the case.

119

I started to walk home.

I thought hard about the stamp.

I knew that Annie and Rosamond
saw the stamp at Claude's house.

Then it rained for a long time.

I knew that after the rain stopped,
Pip saw the stamp, too.

I knew the stamp had been
in Claude's house.

How did it get out, where was it?

There are two sides to every stamp.

Should I think about the sticky side or about the dinosaur side?

"Think sticky," I said to Sludge.

Sludge had not been much help — or had he?

Sludge had wanted to lick the sticky side of a stamp.

That would have made the stamp wet and very sticky.

A very sticky stamp . . . sticks!

All at once I knew that Sludge was
a great detective.

He knew that the sticky side
of the stamp could be important.

I knew that anything wet
would make a stamp sticky.

When Annie and Rosamond went
to Claude's house, it was not raining.

But when Pip went to Claude's
house, it had been raining and stopped.

I thought of puddles.

I thought of Pip walking in them.

I went out and walked in a puddle.
Then I went back inside and walked on the sticky side of a stamp.
The stamp was now on my shoe!
It didn't come off!
The same thing must have happened to the dinosaur stamp and Pip's shoe.
I had to see Pip's shoes.

Sludge and I went to Pip's house.
He had on slippers.
"Where are your shoes?" I asked.

Pip said, "My shoes were all wet.
After I looked at Claude's stamps,
I went to Rosamond's sale.
I gave her my wet shoes
for these slippers."

"Thank you," I said.

Sludge and I went back
to Rosamond's sale.

Rosamond came over.

"I want Pip's shoes," I said.

"Annie has them," Rosamond said.

Sludge and I ran to Annie's house.

I saw two shoes.

Fang had one of them.

"Are these Pip's shoes?" I asked.

"They were," Annie said.

I, Nate the Great, looked
at the shoe that Fang had.
Something little was sticking to it.
At last I had found the stamp.
But I, Nate the Great, knew
that I had to get it, too.
I thought fast.
"Show me Fang's dinosaur smile,"
I said.

"Smile, Fang," Annie said.

Fang smiled.

The shoe fell.

I got it.

I, Nate the Great, got the stamp off.

The case was finished.

Sludge and I took
the dinosaur stamp to Claude's house.
The stamp was sticky,
but Claude was happy to get it.

Sludge and I walked home.
We did not walk in the puddles.

Summary Questions

Nate found Claude's stamp.

These questions will help you tell how he did it.

1. Think about the different things Nate did to find the stamp.
   What things helped him find it?
   What things did not help him?
2. How did Sludge and Fang help Nate find the stamp?
3. Was Nate a good detective?
   What makes you think that?

The Reading and Writing Connection

Claude liked to save stamps.

He was very happy when Nate found his missing dinosaur stamp.

If people want to say "Thank-you," they sometimes write a note.

Write a thank you note from Claude to Nate.

The words in the box can help you.

happy	been	wet	shoe
puddle	slippers	off	

The Dinosaurs' Dinner

by Dennis Lee

Allosaurus, stegosaurus,
Brontosaurus too,
All went off for dinner at the
Dinosaur zoo;

Along came the waiter, called
Tyrannosaurus Rex,
Gobbled up the table
'Cause they wouldn't pay
    their checks.

The Main Idea

When you read a story, you need to think about which sentence tells what all the other sentences are about.

That sentence is called the main idea.

Read this story and think about the main idea.

Ana likes to sail a boat.
Most of all she likes to swim.
Ana likes water sports.

One of these sentences tells
the main idea of the story.

1. Most of all she likes to swim.
2. Ana likes water sports.
3. Ana likes to sail a boat.

Sentence **2** tells the main idea.
It tells what all the other sentences
in the story are about.

Sentences **1** and **3** each tell about
only one water sport that Ana
likes to do.

Now you will read another story.
Think about the main idea.

Mary likes to draw and color.
She uses pencils and pens.
She uses many different colors.
She uses yellow most of all.

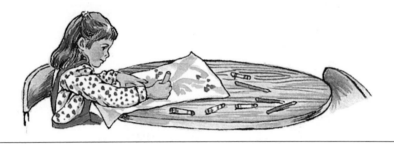

Which sentence tells what all
the other sentences are about?

1. She uses pencils and pens.

2. She uses yellow most of all.

3. Mary likes to draw and color.

Sentence **3** tells the main idea.
Sentences **1** and **2** each tell about
only what Mary uses to draw and color.

Read this story about Will.
Think about the main idea.

Will feeds the hens.
He brings flowers into the house.
Will is a good helper.
He even helps cut the wheat.

Which sentence tells the main idea
of the story? Why?

   1. Will is a good helper.

   2. He even helps cut the wheat.

   3. Will feeds the hens.

Why don't the other sentences
tell the main idea?

The Little Pine Tree

Part 1

In the play:
Little Pine
Big Pine
First Tree
Second Tree
Goat
Wind
Man
Tree Fairy

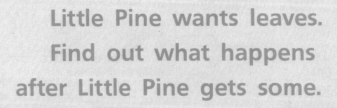

Little Pine wants leaves.
Find out what happens
after Little Pine gets some.

Big Pine: How are you, Little Pine?

Little Pine: I'm very sad, Big Pine.

Big Pine: I'm sorry you are sad.
What's the problem?

Little Pine: I don't want
to be a pine tree.
I want to have leaves.

Big Pine: Why, Little Pine?

Little Pine: It's better to have leaves.
The other trees have fun
when the wind comes by.
The wind can blow and
move the leaves.
That lets the trees sing.
I want to sing, too.

Little Pine: Another thing,
   trees look better with leaves.
   Leaves are so pretty.

Big Pine: But leaves come off.
   Soon the other trees will have
   no leaves at all.

Little Pine: They will get new leaves.

First Tree: I know what you
should do, Little Pine.
When Tree Fairy comes tonight,
ask her to give you leaves.

Little Pine: What a good idea!
After tonight, I'll be a new tree!

First Tree: This is another great day.

Second Tree: Yes, it is.
Look, here comes Wind.

Wind: Why, what has happened?
Little Pine is not here.
I see a new tree!

Little Pine: I'm not a new tree!
I am Little Pine.
I had needles, but now
I have pretty leaves.

141

First Tree: Oh, Tree Fairy
gave you leaves!

Little Pine: That's right.
Please, Wind, make my leaves sing.

Wind: OK, here I go!

Little Pine: This is fun!

Wind: Well, it's time for me to go.
Good-by for now.

Little Pine: Look, here comes a goat.

Goat: Hello, are you new here?

Little Pine: I am Little Pine.
Tree Fairy gave me leaves.
How do you like them?

Goat: Let me eat some and find out.

Little Pine: Don't eat my leaves!

Goat: Oh, these are very good.

Little Pine: Look at me, Goat!
You ate all my leaves.

Goat: They were very good.
Good-by, and thank you.

Big Pine: I'm sorry Goat ate
your leaves, Little Pine.
Maybe it would be better
if you got back your needles.

Little Pine: No! I don't want needles!
Tonight I'll ask for something new.

Summary Questions

These questions will help you tell about Little Pine.

1. Why did Little Pine want leaves?
2. Why was Little Pine still not happy?
3. Should Little Pine ask Tree Fairy for something new? Why or why not?

The Reading and Writing Connection

Little Pine will see Tree Fairy tonight.
Write about how you think Little Pine will look in the morning.
The words in the box can help you.

pine	fairy	pretty	better
blow	wind	goat	sorry

The Little Pine Tree

Part 2

Little Pine still wants leaves.
Find out what makes
Little Pine happy at last.

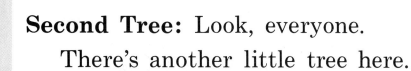

Second Tree: Look, everyone.
　　There's another little tree here.

Big Pine: Can this be Little Pine?

Little Pine: Yes, it is.
　　How do you like my new leaves?
　　Don't I look pretty?
　　They are made of glass.
　　No one will eat glass leaves.

147

Wind: Good morning, Trees!

First Tree: Good morning, Wind.
Look at this new tree.

Wind: How do you do?

Little Pine: You know me, Wind.
I once had needles,
and then I had leaves.
A goat ate the leaves.
But look at these great glass leaves.

Wind: Let me see if they can sing.

Little Pine: Stop, Wind, stop!
  You are blowing too hard!
  You'll break all my glass leaves!

Wind: I'm sorry, Little Pine.
  I had to blow hard or your
  glass leaves wouldn't move.

Little Pine: What am I going to do?
The wind broke all my leaves.

Big Pine: Maybe tonight Tree Fairy
can give you back your needles.

Little Pine: I don't want any needles!
Tonight I'll ask for gold leaves.
Gold leaves won't get eaten,
and they won't be broken.

Little Pine: Take a look at me!

First Tree: Who is calling us?

Second Tree: Who is it?

Little Pine: It's Little Pine.
Look, I have gold leaves!

Man: Are these leaves made of gold?

Little Pine: Yes, aren't they pretty?

Big Pine: He doesn't know
you are talking, Little Pine.

Man: I'll take all these gold leaves.
From now on I can use the gold
to get food for my children.

Little Pine: Don't take my leaves!

Little Pine: I'm so sad.

A goat ate my first leaves.

The wind broke my glass leaves.

The man has taken my gold leaves.

I wish I had my needles back.

But I don't know if Tree Fairy

will give me another wish.

Big Pine: You'll know soon.

Here comes Tree Fairy now.

Tree Fairy: Where are all
your gold leaves, Little Pine?

Little Pine: A man took them.
He said he needed the gold
to get food for his children.

Tree Fairy: I can give you
just one more wish, Little Pine.
What do you want?

Little Pine: I want my pine needles.
May I have them back?

Tree Fairy: Yes, you may.
I'll give them to you right now.
There!

Little Pine: Thank you, Tree Fairy. I have my needles back, and it's great to be a pine tree again!

Story Wrap-up

Summary Questions

Each new wish gave Little Pine a new problem!

These questions will help you tell why Little Pine was happy at last.

1. What things did Little Pine wish for?
2. Why wasn't Little Pine happy with any of them?
3. What did Little Pine decide was the best thing to have? Why?
4. Do you think Little Pine will ever wish to be different again? Why or why not?

The Reading and Writing Connection

Here is the beginning of a play about Little Pine and a tree named Tiny Pine.

Little Pine: How are you, Tiny Pine?

Tiny Pine: I am very sad.

Finish the play.
Write about why Tiny Pine is sad and how Little Pine helps Tiny Pine.
The words in the box may help you.

glass	**fairy**	**wish**	**break**
gold	**pretty**	**sorry**	

Autumn Wind

by Helen Howland Prommel

Blow, wind —
    Blow the leaves along!
Blow, wind —
    Sing your little song!

Rattle all the red leaves,
    Shake them till they fall,
But make the brittle brown leaves
    Rattle best of all.

Blow, wind —
    Blow the leaves away
Sing a little song, wind,
    For an autumn day!

Magazine Wrap-up

What Did They Do?

1. What problem did Harriet, Claude, and Little Pine each have? How did they work out their problems?

2. Why did Harriet help Mrs. Hoozit? Why did Nate help Claude?

Writing About Someone

What if someone in this part
of the book could be your friend?
Name the friend you would want.
Write some sentences telling why
you would want that friend.

Books to Enjoy

Ottie and the Star by Laura Jean Allen
See what happens when Ottie tries
to get a star to play with.

Henrietta Goes to the Fair by Syd Hoff
Henrietta the hen gets Farmer Gray
a surprise when she goes to the fair.

Nate the Great and the Phony Clue
by Marjorie Weinman Sharmat
Here's another special case for Nate.

Carousels

Magazine Three

Contents

Stories

166 **What Mary Jo Shared**
Janice May Udry

188 **Clyde Monster**
Robert L. Crowe

208 **Good As New**
Barbara Douglass

228 Medallion Selection:
The Man and His Caps

164

Article

203 **Animal Homes**

Poems

187 **Umbrellas**
Barbara Juster Esbensen

201 **Night Comes**
Beatrice Schenk de Regniers

Skill: Decoding Strategy
224 **Reading New Words**

Vocabulary
202 **Describing Words**

242 Magazine Wrap-up

244 **Picture Dictionary**

253 **Student Handbook**

What Mary Jo Shared

by Janice May Udry

Part 1

Mary Jo is shy, but she does want
to share something at school.
See what Mary Jo wants to share.

When it was Sharing Time at school,
Mary Jo wouldn't share anything.

She was too shy to tell
the other children about anything.

She didn't think they would listen
to her.

Miss Willet was the teacher.
She would ask, "Mary Jo, do you
have something to share with us?"

Mary Jo would shake her head.
Then she would look down.

"Why don't you share anything?"
her friend Laurie would ask.

"I will some day," Mary Jo would say.
"I just don't want to today."
Mary Jo did want to share,
but she was too shy.

At night her father would ask,
"Did you share something today?"

Mary Jo would shake her head
and say, "Not today."

One day it was raining hard.

Mary Jo thought, "I'll share my new umbrella.

I can't wait to get to school."

Mary Jo ate her breakfast as fast as she could.

Then she put on her raincoat and got out her blue umbrella.

This was her very first umbrella.

When Mary Jo got to school,
she saw many other umbrellas!

"Just about everyone in my room
has an umbrella," thought Mary Jo.

"Maybe my blue umbrella isn't
a good thing to share after all."

At Sharing Time, Miss Willet asked,
"Mary Jo, do you have something
to share this morning?"

Mary Jo shook her head
and looked down.

The next day Mary Jo and
her brother found a grasshopper.

They got a jar for the grasshopper
and made some holes in the jar.

"I'll share the grasshopper!"
thought Mary Jo.

So she took it to school.

When Mary Jo got to school, she saw the boys and girls looking at something.

She went to see what the boys and girls were looking at.

"Jimmy's got three grasshoppers!" said Laurie.

"He found them all by himself."

Mary Jo thought about her one
grasshopper — and how her brother
had helped find it.

"I don't think I'll share
my grasshopper after all," she thought.

At Sharing Time, the teacher asked,
"Mary Jo, do you have something
to share this morning?"

Mary Jo just shook her head.

All the other boys and girls
in Miss Willet's room shared things.
They shared their books.
They shared their letters.
Sometimes they shared things
they found in the woods.

Now Mary Jo wanted
to share something very much.
She wanted to share something
that no one in her room had shared.

Summary Questions

These questions will help you tell about Mary Jo's problem.

1. What showed that Mary Jo was shy?
2. Why didn't Mary Jo share the umbrella or the grasshopper?
3. What would you tell Mary Jo to help her with her problem?

The Reading and Writing Connection

The words in the box name two things Mary Jo thought of sharing.

blue umbrella   grasshopper

Write what Mary Jo would have said if she had shared one of these things.

175

What Mary Jo Shared

by Janice May Udry

Part 2

At last Mary Jo thinks of something
that no one in her room has shared.
How will Mary Jo feel
after she shares it?

One night Mary Jo's father asked, "Did you share something today?"

Mary Jo said, "Not today."

Just then she thought of something! "Could you go to school with me tomorrow?" she asked her father.

"Tomorrow?" asked her father.
"Why, yes, I think I can."

"Good!" said Mary Jo.
"Then you can come and listen
as I share something."

"All right," said her father.
"What are you going to share?"

"Wait and see," said Mary Jo.

The next morning, Mary Jo and
her father went to school.

The teacher said she was very happy
Mary Jo's father had come to school.

"I have something to share today,"
said Mary Jo.

"Great!" Miss Willet said.

At Sharing Time, Miss Willet asked,
"Who has something to share?"

Mary Jo put up her hand.
"I do," she said.
She went to the front of the room.

"This morning I am going to share
my father," Mary Jo said.

All the children smiled.
Mary Jo's father smiled, too,
and waited to be shared.

"This is my father," said Mary Jo.
"His name is Mr. William Wood.
He and my mother have
three children."

Jimmy put up his hand.
"My father grew up in the West,"
said Jimmy.
"Where did your father come from?"

"My father is from the West, too,"
said Mary Jo.

"He is a teacher.

He likes to read and to go fishing."

"So does my father!" said one girl.

"My dad is a teacher, too," said a boy.

They *all* wanted to share
their fathers!

Miss Willet said, "Children, Mary Jo
is sharing her father today."

"When my father was little," Mary Jo
went on, "he wasn't good all the time."

A girl asked, "What did he do?"

"Well," said Mary Jo, "one day he ate
some of the biscuits his mother
had made for a school supper."

Then Mary Jo said,
"Now my father will talk to you."

Then from the front of the room,
Mr. Wood started to talk.

He smiled and talked about
how much he liked coming
to Miss Willet's room.

Mary Jo felt good.
At last she had shared something
that no one in her room had shared.

Summary Questions

At last Mary Jo shared something. The questions will help you tell what happened.

1. What did Mary Jo share?
   Why didn't she feel shy this time?
2. How did the other children feel about what Mary Jo shared?
   How do you know that?
3. How do you think Mary Jo's father felt about being shared? Why?
4. Do you think that Mary Jo will share other things from now on?
   Why or why not?

The Reading and Writing Connection

Jimmy asked Mary Jo a question about her father.

Make believe that you were in Miss Willet's room.

What would you have asked Mary Jo about her father?

Write some of the questions.

The words in the box may help you.

West front shy teacher father

Umbrellas

by Barbara Juster Esbensen

Umbrellas bloom
Along our street
Like flowers on a stem.
And almost everyone
I meet
Is holding one of them.

Under my umbrella-top,
Splashing through the town,
I wonder why the tulips
Hold umbrellas
Up-side-down!

Clyde Monster

by Robert L. Crowe

Clyde Monster is too scared to go into his cave.

Find out if Mother and Father can help Clyde.

Clyde wasn't very big,
but he was ugly.

And he was getting uglier every day.

He lived in the woods
with his mother and father.

Father Monster was a big monster.

He was very ugly, which was good.

Mother Monster was even uglier,
which was better.

Monsters laugh at pretty monsters.

All in all, Clyde and his mother and
his father were lovely monsters —
as monsters go.

All day Clyde played in the woods doing lovely monster things.

He liked to make big holes and he liked to walk into things.

At night Clyde lived in a cave.

But then one night he would not go into his cave.

"Why?" asked his mother.
"Why won't you go into your cave?"

"I'm scared of the dark," said Clyde.

"Scared?" asked his father.
"What are you scared of?"

"People," said Clyde.
"I'm scared there are people
in the cave who will get me."

"That's silly," said his father.
"Come, I'll show you.
   There.
   Did you see any people?"

"No," said Clyde,
"but people can hide.
   They may be hiding under a rock.
   They will jump out and get me
after I go to sleep."

"That is silly," said his mother.
"There are no people here.
   Even if there were,
they wouldn't get you."

"They wouldn't?" asked Clyde.

"No," said his mother.
"Would you ever hide in the dark?
   Would you hide under a bed
to scare a boy or a girl?"

"No!" said Clyde.
"I would never do a thing like that!"

"Well, people won't hide
and scare you," said his father.
"It just so happens that
monsters and people have made a deal.
Monsters never scare people —
and people never scare monsters."

"Are you sure?" Clyde asked.

"Very sure," said his mother.
"Do you know of any monsters
that were ever scared by people?"

"No," said Clyde.

"Do you know of any people who
were ever scared by monsters?"
asked his mother.

"No," Clyde said.

"There!" said his mother.
"Now it's time for bed."

"And," said his father, "I don't want you to talk anymore about being scared by people."

"OK," said Clyde as he went into the cave.

"But could you leave the rock open just a little?"

Summary Questions

Clyde Monster was scared.
The questions will help you tell
what happened.

1. Why was Clyde scared?
2. Do you think Mother and Father helped Clyde? Why or why not?
3. Why do you think Clyde asked Father to leave the rock open?
4. What do you think Clyde would tell a girl or a boy who was scared of monsters?

The Reading and Writing Connection

Father, Mother, and Clyde were very lovely monsters – as monsters go.

They did lovely monster things.

Draw some monsters.

Write about them.

Tell what your monsters look like and what they would do.

The words in the box can help you.

ugly	open	never	deal
people	cave	sure	hide

Night Comes

by Beatrice Schenk de Regniers

Night comes
leaking
out of the sky.
Stars come
peeking.
Moon comes
sneaking,
silvery-sly.
Who is
shaking,
shivery-
quaking?
Who is afraid
of the night?

Not I.

Describing Words

These words are describing words.

happy   pretty   blue

Describing words can tell how something looks.

Read these sentences.

1. The monster has shoes.
2. The monster has blue shoes.

The word **blue** tells how the shoes look.

Tell some more about the monster.
Use describing words that tell how the monster looks.

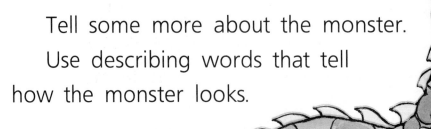

Animal
Homes

Have you ever thought about
where animals live?

Animals live in many places.

Caves, trees, and holes under
the ground can be animal homes.

In the daytime, some bats rest
and sleep in caves.

When it starts to get dark,
they go out to get food.

There are birds that live
in caves, too.

Like the bats, these birds
go out of the cave to get food.

One animal that lives in a tree
is a squirrel.

You can sometimes see a squirrel
as it runs from one tree to another.

There are many kinds of owls
that live in trees.

Many of these owls rest
in the daytime and fly about
at night.

Moles live underground.
They don't come out much.
They get their food under the ground.

A grasshopper mouse lives
underground, too.
It comes out at night to get food.

There are other animals that live
in caves, in trees, or under the ground.
You may want to find out about
some other animals that live
in these kinds of animal homes.

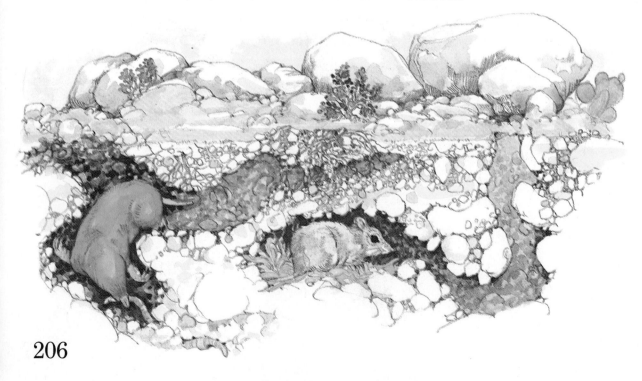

Summary Questions

The questions will help you tell about animal homes.

1. What are three kinds of animal homes?
2. What animals live in each kind?
3. Which animal home do you think would be fun to live in? Why?

The Reading and Writing Connection

Make believe you are an animal.

bat	**squirrel**	**bird**	**mole**
owl	**grasshopper**	**mouse**	

Write about yourself, but don't tell which animal you are.

See if a friend can name the animal.

Good As New

by Barbara Douglass

Grady has a teddy bear that needs to be fixed.
Find out if Grandpa can fix it.

I thought Grandpa could fix anything.

But then one day K.C. came over.

He started crying as soon as
his father went away.

Nobody could make him happy,
not even Grandpa.

The only thing K.C. wanted was
my bear.

I said, "Huh-uh. Nobody plays
with my bear but me."

K.C. cried some more.

Mom said, "Grady, do you think
K.C. wishes he had *his* bear?"

Dad said, "Do you think he
would feel better if you just let him
hold your bear?"

Before I could say,
"OK, you can HOLD him,"
K.C. pulled my bear away from me.

But K.C. didn't just hold him.
He pulled my bear by the ears.
He got him sticky.
He tried to feed him to the dog.
Dad made K.C. stop.

So K.C. took my bear outside.
He got my bear all wet and dirty.
Dad made him stop that, too.

At last K.C. went home.
My bear was a mess.

Mom said, "Please, don't bring it
in the house."

Dad said, "I'm sorry, Grady.
I'll get you a new bear."

I said, "I don't want a new bear.
I want this one fixed."
Mom and Dad shook their heads.

But Grandpa said,
"Never you mind now, Grady.
I can fix that bear so he'll be
as good as new in no time."

Grandpa and I sat down
to fix my bear.

But when I saw what he was going
to do, I said, *"Wait*, Grandpa.

Are you sure you can fix my bear?"

"Sure I can," said Grandpa.

Then he opened up my bear —
and then — he pulled out
all the stuffing!

My bear's head went flat.
Soon he was wrinkled up all over.
I said, "Grandpa, are you sure
this is the right way to fix my bear?"
Grandpa just went on working.

I said, "Grandpa! Are you sure?"

He said, "Never you mind now.
We'll have this bear as good as new
in no time."

We went into the kitchen
where Grandpa scrubbed my bear.

First he scrubbed the legs.

Then he scrubbed the head and
the arms.

He even scrubbed the ears.

But my bear was still dirty.

So Grandpa scrubbed again.

But this time he scrubbed too hard.

Both the ears fell off.

I said, "Grandpa! I'm not sure
this is the right way to fix my bear."

"Never you mind now," Grandpa said.
"He'll be as good as new in no time."

At last Grandpa shook out my bear.
I told him, "Grandpa, this bear's
not so good if it's all flat and
wrinkled and it hasn't got any ears!"

"Never you mind now," Grandpa said.
"I have to go get new stuffing.
Anyone want to come with me?"
I did.

When we got back home, my bear
was still all flat and wrinkled.

I said, "Grandpa, are you sure..."

I think you know what Grandpa said.

Then he sat down and put
new stuffing into my bear.

He put stuffing in the arms.

He put stuffing in the legs.

He put stuffing in the head.

But my bear still looked flat.

So Grandpa went on stuffing.

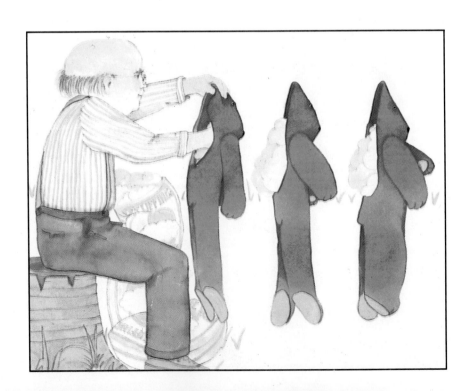

At last Grandpa said, "There..."

But I said, "Wait, Grandpa!
He isn't dirty anymore and he
isn't flat or wrinkled, but he still
doesn't look so good without..."

"Without what?" my grandpa asked.

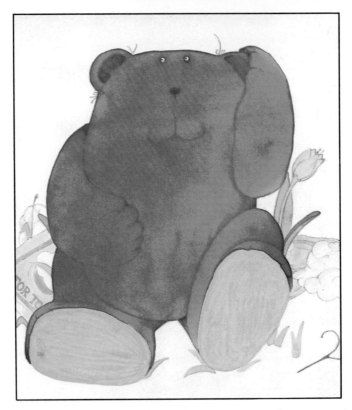

"Never you mind," Grandpa said.
"I can fix that, too."
So he did.

Then he asked, "Is that better?"
I looked at my bear in the front,
in the back, and all over.

"Grandpa," I said at last,
"I thought you could fix anything.
    But this bear isn't good as new."

Grandpa looked kind of sad.

"It's *better* than new!"
I shouted, laughing.
And I gave him my best bear hug.

Now whenever K.C.
comes over, Grandpa and I take
my good-as-new bear, and we go out
for a long, long walk.

Story Wrap-up

Summary Questions

Grady's bear was a mess!
The questions will help you
tell what happened.

1. Why do you think K.C. made a mess of Grady's teddy bear?
2. How did Grandpa fix Grady's bear?
3. How did Grady feel when Grandpa was fixing the bear? Why?
4. What did Grady mean when he said the bear was "better than new"?
5. Do you think Grady would let you play with his bear? Why or why not?

The Reading and Writing Connection

Here are some of the ways that Grady's bear looked in the story.

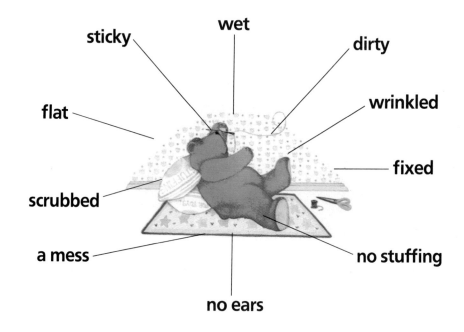

Draw a picture of Grady's bear when K.C. was finished with it.

Draw a picture of Grady's bear when Grandpa was finished with it.

Write about each picture.

Reading New Words

Dear Laurie,

I had to go to the store with my dad.
We decided to get some chicken
to eat for supper.

Rosamond

We decided
to get some _____
to eat for supper.

Laurie is trying to read a note
that her friend has left for her.
But Laurie has come to a word
that she has never read before.
What should Laurie do
to read that word?

Laurie should think about the sense
of the words that she can read.

She knows that Rosamond
had to go to the store.

Laurie knows that Rosamond is getting
something to eat for supper.

Laurie should also think about
the sounds for the letters in the new word.

chicken

   If Laurie thinks about the sense
of the words that she can read,
about the sounds for the letters in the
new word, and about what makes sense
in the sentence, she can read the word.

   Now look back at the note and see
if you can read the word that tells
what Rosamond and her dad will eat.

Reading New Words

1. Think about the sense of the words you can read.

2. Think about the sounds for the letters in the new word.

3. Think about what makes sense in the sentence.

Read these sentences.

The words in dark letters may be new to you.

Use what you know about reading new words to help you read them.

1. He moved a **finger** on his left hand.

2. Her silly **jokes** don't make sense.

3. I also scrubbed the dirty **dishes.**

***The Man
and His Caps***

a folktale

**pictures by
Jane Dyer**

This is a story
about a man who has
caps for sale.

He has many caps,
and he wears them all
on his head.

One day all
but one of the man's
caps are missing.

Find out if he
gets back his caps.

228

The Man and His Caps

a folktale

Once there was a man who had many caps for sale.

He had the caps on his head.

First he had on his old brown cap.

On top of the brown cap, he had orange caps.

On top of the orange caps, he had blue caps.

On top of the blue caps, he had yellow caps.

And on the very top, he had red caps.

Every day the man would walk up one street and down another.

He would call, "Caps for sale! Caps for sale!"

One day no one wanted a cap,
not even a red one.

"Well," thought the man,
"I may as well get some sleep."

So he walked off and found
a big tree to sleep under.

The man made sure all his caps
were in place, then he went to sleep.

When the man got up,
he put up his hand to see if his caps
were all in place.

All he had was his old brown cap!

He looked in front of him.
No caps.
He looked to the right of him.
No caps.
He looked to the left of him.
No caps.
He looked all around the tree.
No caps.

The man looked up in the tree.
There he saw monkeys, and
each monkey had a cap on its head!

"You monkeys, you!" the man
shouted, shaking his right hand.
"You give me back my caps."

The monkeys only shook
their hands back at him
and shouted, "Tsk! Tsk! Tsk!"

"You monkeys, you!" the man shouted, shaking his left hand at them.

"You give me back my caps."

The monkeys only shook their hands back at him and shouted, "Tsk! Tsk! Tsk!"

"You monkeys, you!" the man
shouted as he stamped his right foot.
"You give me back my caps."

The monkeys only shouted back
at him, "Tsk! Tsk! Tsk!"

"You monkeys, you!" the man said
as he stamped his left foot.
"Give me back my caps."

The monkeys only called back,
"Tsk! Tsk! Tsk!"

Now the man was very angry.

He was so angry that he took off his old brown cap and threw it down.

Then each monkey took off its cap and threw it down!

So the man got all
his caps and put them back
on his head.

First he put on
his old brown cap.
On top of the brown cap,
he put his orange caps.
On top of the orange caps,
he put his blue caps.
On top of the blue caps,
he put his yellow caps.
And on the very top,
he put his red caps.

Then he went back
to walking up and down
the streets calling,
"Caps for sale! Caps for sale!"

Summary Questions

The questions will help you tell what happened to the man, the monkeys, and the caps.

1. Why do you think the monkeys took the man's caps?
2. What things helped you know that the man was angry?
3. How did being angry help the man get back his caps?
4. What would you tell the man to do the next time he decides to sleep under a tree?

The Reading and Writing Connection

The monkeys left the old brown cap on top of the man's head.

Write another story about the man and his caps.

In your story, have the monkeys take the brown cap, too.

Tell how the man gets his caps back now.

The words in the box can help you.

old	**angry**	**caps**
monkeys	**threw**	**wears**

Magazine Wrap-up

Looking Back

1. Mary Jo, Clyde, and Grady
    each had a family.
    Tell about each family.

2. Mary Jo, Clyde, Grady,
    and the man who had caps
    all had problems.
    Who worked out their problems
    without help from anyone?
    Who got help from others?

242

Writing a Note

Write the name of the one you liked most in this part of the book.
Write a note to that someone.

Books to Enjoy

Follow Me by Mordicai Gerstein
See what happens when some ducks get lost on their way home.

Curious George Flies a Kite
by Margaret Rey
Here's a funny story about a monkey who tries to fly a kite and to fish.

Molly and the Slow Teeth by Pat Ross
Molly is waiting for her first tooth to come out.
Find out what happens to her.

Picture Dictionary

Aa

alphabet
Do you know the letters
of the **alphabet**?

Bb

blue
Color the pond **blue.**

brother
Pam has a big **brother.**

Cc

colors
What **colors** are in your picture?

Dd

different

Things can be the same,
or they can be **different.**

dinosaur

A **dinosaur** was
a big animal.

Ee

ears

Use your **ears** to listen.

Ff

fast

The fox can run **fast.**

flower

Who planted that **flower**?

Gg

garden
Water the plants
in the **garden.**

girls
The boys and **girls** played.

glass
May I have a **glass** of water?

ground
Some animals live
under the **ground.**

Hh

hand
If you want help, put up your **hand.**

happy
We smile when we feel **happy.**

Ii

important

Listen for **important** ideas.

Ll

letters

How many **letters** are in your name?

Mm

meaning

What is the **meaning** of that word?

morning

We get out of bed in the **morning.**

move

Max will **move** to a new home.

Nn

never

We **never** found the lost key.

note

Dad wrote a **note.**

Oo

off

The cat jumped
off the fence.

old

Is this book **old** or new?

open

Please **open** the window.

Pp

people
Five **people** are in the family.

pretty
Lee made a **pretty** picture.

pulled
Tina **pulled**
on the kite.

Rr

race
Who will win the **race**?

raining
It is **raining,** so come
in the house.

right
Are you feeling all **right**?

same

These two rabbits are the **same.**

sentences

Use **sentences** when you write.

shoe

The **shoe** is too big.

shouted

"Help! Help!" **shouted** the boy.

smile

We like to laugh and **smile.**

special

Tell us about a **special** time.

stick

The **stick** fell from the tree.

Tt

talk

The friends like to **talk.**

teacher

The **teacher** helped the children.

told

Dad **told** a long story.

took

Who **took** the book?

Uu

under

The dog is
under the table.

Uu

use

Can you **use** some help?

Ww

warm

The day is nice and **warm.**

water

Plants need **water.**

wind

A kite will fly in the **wind.**

write

Mary can **write** her name.

Yy

yellow

The paint is **yellow.**

Read
Write
Listen
Speak

Read

Reading Unknown Words

When you come to a new word —

- Read to the end of the sentence.
- Think about what the words are saying.
- Think about the sounds for the letters.

Sounds You Know

b c d f g h j k l m n p r s t v w x y

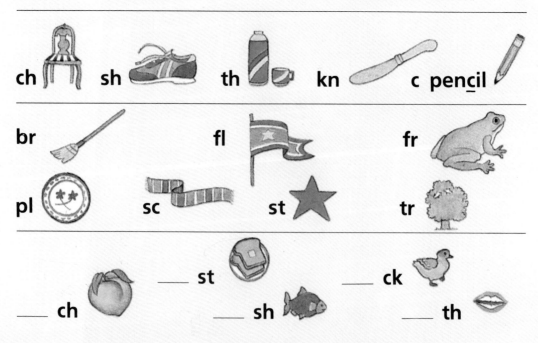

ch   sh   th   kn   c pen<u>c</u>il

br   fl   fr

pl   sc   st   tr

___ st   ___ ck

___ ch   ___ sh   ___ th

More Sounds You Know – Vowels

short **a**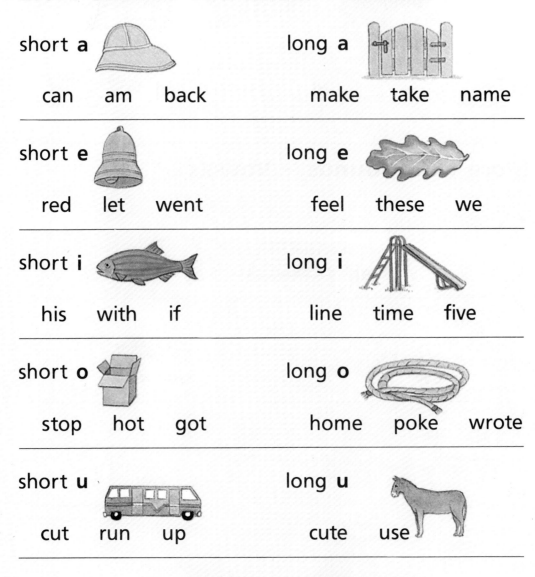

can   am   back

long **a**

make   take   name

short **e**

red   let   went

long **e**

feel   these   we

short **i**

his   with   if

long **i**

line   time   five

short **o**

stop   hot   got

long **o**

home   poke   wrote

short **u**

cut   run   up

long **u**

cute   use

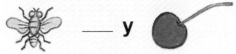

— **y**

255

New Sounds

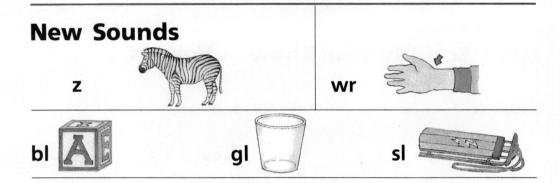

z

wr

bl

gl

sl

More New Sounds – Vowels

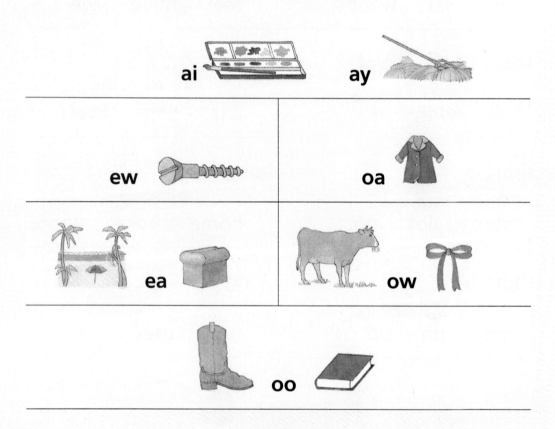

ai

ay

ew

oa

ea

ow

oo

The Writing Process

1 Prewriting

- Before you begin to write, think of some story ideas.

- Make a list or draw pictures of your ideas.

- Choose one idea.

my wish

a monster in town

the talking mouse

- Think about your idea.

   What will happen at the beginning
   of the story?
   What will happen in the middle?
   What will happen at the end?
- Draw pictures to show what happens.

② Write a First Draft

● Write sentences to tell
  what happens in the story.

Once there was a monster.
all the peple ran away
from him.
One boy talked to the monster.
The monster was friendly

3 Revise

- Read your story.
- Add words and sentences to tell more.
- Read your story to a friend. What does your friend think?
- Change your story some more to make it even better.

Once there was a big orange monster.
He came down the street.
all the peple ran away from him.
One boy was not scared. He talked to the monster.
The monster was friendly

4 Proofread

- Look at the story one more time.
- Fix any mistakes.

  Does each sentence begin with a capital letter?

  Does each sentence end with the correct mark?

  Is each word spelled correctly?

Once there was a ^big orange^ monster.
^A all the ~~peple~~ ^people^ ran away
from him. ^He came down the street.^
One boy ^was not scared. He^ talked to the monster.
The monster was friendly.

❺ Publish

- Copy your story neatly.
- Put your story where other people can read it.

The Monster
     by Brian K.
Once there was a big
orange monster.
   He came down the street.
   All the people ran away
from him.
   One boy was not scared.
   He talked to the monster.
   The monster was friendly.

Listen and Speak

Listening

Listen to follow directions.

- Listen to all the steps.
- Listen for the words **first, next,** and **last.**
- Ask questions at the end.

Speaking

Give a talk.

- Plan what you will say.
- Tell about something you know.
- Tell about something you have done.
- Speak loudly and clearly.
- Look at the group.